PRAYERS OF THE SOCIAL AWAKENING

PRAYERS OF THE SOCIAL AWAKENING

BY

WALTER RAUSCHENBUSCH

Author of "Christianity and the Social Crisis"

Wipf & Stock

PUBLISHERS

Eugene, Oregon

Wipf and Stock Publishers
199 W 8th Ave, Suite 3
Eugene, OR 97401

Prayers of the Social Awakening
By Rauschenbusch, Walter
ISBN: 1-59244-918-2
Publication date 10/4/2004
Previously published by The Pilgrim Press, 1910

TO

MY FRIENDS

AMONG WHOM ARE AFFECTIONATELY
MENTIONED
EDMUND AND CAROLYN LYON
TWO REAL FRIENDS

CONTENTS

PREFACE

THE new social purpose, which has laid its masterful grasp on modern life and thought, is enlarging and transforming our whole conception of the meaning of Christianity. The Bible and all past history speak a new and living language. The life of men about us stands out with an open-air color and vividness which it never had in the dusky solemnity of the older theological views about humanity. All the older tasks of church life have taken on a new significance, and vastly larger tasks are emerging as from the mists of a new morning.

Many ideas that used to seem fundamental and satisfying seem strangely narrow and trivial in this greater world of God. Some of the old religious appeals have utterly lost their power over us. But there are others, unknown to our fathers, which kindle religious passions of wonderful intensity and purity. The wrongs and sufferings of the people and the vision of a righteous and brotherly social life awaken an almost painful compassion and longing, and these feelings are more essentially Christian than most of the fears and desires of religion in the past. Social Christianity is adding to the variety of religious experience, and is creating a new type of Christian man who bears a striking family likeness to Jesus of Galilee.

These new religious emotions ought to find conscious and social expression. But the Church, which has brought down so rich an equipment from the past for the culture of individual religion, is poverty-stricken in face of this new need. The ordinary church hymnal rarely contains more than two or three hymns in which the triumphant chords of the social hope are struck. Our liturgies and devotional manuals offer very little that is fit to enrich and purify the social thoughts and feelings.

Even men who have absorbed the social ideals are apt to move within the traditional round in public prayer. The language of prayer always clings to the antique for the sake of dignity, and plain reference to modern facts and contrivances jars the ear. So we are inclined to follow the broad avenues beaten by the feet of many generations when we approach God. We need to blaze new paths to God for the feet of modern men.

I offer this little book as an attempt in that direction. So far as I know, it is the first of its kind, and it is likely to meet the sort of objections which every pioneering venture in religion has to encounter. I realize keenly the limitations which are inevitable when one mind is to furnish a vehicle for the most intimate spiritual thoughts of others. But whenever a great movement stirs the deeper passions of men, a common soul is born, and all who feel the throb of the new age have such unity of thought and aim and feeling, that the utterance of one man may in a measure be the voice of all. A number of the prayers in this collection were published month by month in the American Magazine. The response to them showed that there is a great craving for a religious expression of the new social feeling.

If the moral demands of our higher social thought could find adequate expression in prayer, it would have a profound influence on the social movement. Many good men have given up the habit of praying, partly through philosophical doubt, partly because they feel that it is useless or even harmful to their spiritual nature. Prayer in the past, like the hiss of escaping steam, has often dissipated moral energy. But prayer before battle is another thing. That has been the greatest breeder of revolutionary heroism in history. All our bravest desires stiffen into fighting temper when they are affirmed before God.

Public prayer, too, may carry farther than we know. When men are in the presence of God, the best that is in them has a breathing-space. Then, if ever, we feel the vanity and shamefulness of much that society calls proper and necessary. If we had more prayer in common on the sins of modern society, there would be more social repentance and less angry resistance to the demands of justice and mercy.

And if the effect of our prayers goes beyond our own personality; if there is a center of the spiritual universe in whom our spirits join and have their being; and if the mysterious call of our souls somehow reaches and moves God, so that our longings come back from him in a wave of divine assent which assures their ultimate fulfilment — then it may mean more than any man knows to set Christendom praying on our social problems.

. . . .

I am indebted to my friend, Mr. Mornay Williams, who has long been the president of the New York Juvenile Asylum, for the prayers "For the Children of the Street," and "For Judges." A number of my friends have aided this book more than I can say by their advice and suggestions, and have made it in a measure the work of a group. I shall welcome suggestions from any one which would improve or enrich this little collection in some future edition.

Permission is gladly given to reprint single prayers in newspapers, church programs, and similar publications, provided no change is made in the wording. I should be glad if proper acknowledgment were made in every case so that the attention of others may be called to this little book and its usefulness increased.

WALTER RAUSCHENBUSCH.

Rochester, N. Y.

INTRODUCTORY: THE SOCIAL MEANING OF THE LORD'S PRAYER

THE Lord's Prayer is recognized as the purest expression of the mind of Jesus. It crystallizes his thoughts. It conveys the atmosphere of his childlike trust in the Father. It gives proof of the transparent clearness and peace of his soul.

It first took shape as a protest against the wordy flattery with which men tried to wheedle their gods. He demanded simplicity and sincerity in all expressions of religion, and offered this as an example of the straightforwardness with which men might deal with their Father. Hence the brevity and conciseness of it:

"In praying use not vain repetitions, as the Gentiles do: for they think that they shall be heard for their much speaking. Be not therefore like unto them: for your Father knoweth what things ye have need of before ye ask him. After this manner therefore pray ye:

Our Father who art in heaven,
Hallowed be thy name.

Thy kingdom come.

Thy will be done, as in heaven, so on earth.

Give us this day our daily bread.

And forgive us our debts, as we also have forgiven our debtors.

And bring us not into temptation, but deliver us from the evil one."

Matthew 6: 7–13. (American Revision.)

The Lord's Prayer is so familiar to us that few have stopped to understand it. The general tragedy of misunderstanding which has followed Jesus throughout the centuries has frustrated the purpose of his model prayer also. He gave it to stop vain repetitions, and it has been turned into a contrivance for incessant repetition.

The churches have employed it for their ecclesiastical ritual. Yet it is not ecclesiastical. There is no hint in it of the Church, the ministry, the doctrines of theology, or the sacraments — though the Latin Vulgate has turned the petition for the daily bread into a prayer for the "super-substantial bread" of the sacrament.

It has also been used for the devotions of the personal religious life. It is, indeed, profoundly personal. But its deepest significance for the individual is revealed only when he dedicates his personality to the vaster purposes of the kingdom of God, and approaches all his personal problems from that point of view. Then he enters both into the real meaning of the Lord's Prayer, and into the spirit of the Lord himself.

The Lord's Prayer is part of the heritage of social Christianity which has been appropriated by men who have had little sympathy with its social spirit. It belongs to the equipment of the soldiers of the kingdom of God. I wish to claim it here as the great charter of all social prayers.

When he bade us say, "Our Father," Jesus spoke from that consciousness of human solidarity which was a matter of course in all his thinking. He compels us to clasp hands in spirit with all our brothers and thus to approach the Father together. This rules out all selfish isolation in religion. Before God no man stands alone. Before the All-seeing he is surrounded by the spiritual throng of all to whom he stands related near and far, all whom he loves or hates, whom he serves or oppresses, whom he wrongs or saves. We are one with our fellow-men in all our needs. We are one in our sin and our salvation. To recognize that oneness is the first step toward praying the Lord's Prayer aright. That recognition is also the foundation of social Christianity.

The three petitions with which the prayer begins express the great desire which was fundamental in the heart and mind of Jesus: "Hallowed be thy name. Thy kingdom come. Thy will be done, as in heaven, so on earth." Together they express his yearning faith in the possibility of a reign of God on earth in which his name shall be hallowed and his will be done. They look forward to the ultimate perfection of the common life of humanity on this earth, and pray for the divine revolution which is to bring that about.

There is no request here that we be saved from earthliness and go to heaven which has been the great object of churchly religion. We pray here that heaven may be duplicated on earth through the moral and spiritual transformation of humanity, both in its personal units and its corporate life. No form of religion has ever interpreted this prayer aright which did not have a loving understanding for the plain daily relations of men, and a living faith in their possible spiritual nobility.

And no man has outgrown the crude selfishness of religious immaturity who has not followed Jesus in setting this desire for the social salvation of mankind ahead of all personal desires. The desire for the kingdom of God precedes and outranks everything else in religion, and forms the tacit presupposition of all our wishes for ourselves. In fact, no one has a clear right to ask for bread for his body or strength for his soul, unless he has identified his will with this all-embracing purpose of God, and intends to use the vitality of body and soul in the attainment of that end.

With that understanding we can say that the remaining petitions deal with personal needs.

Among these the prayer for the daily bread takes first place. Jesus was never as "spiritual" as some of his later followers. He never forgot or belittled the elemental need of men for bread. The fundamental place which he gives to this petition is a recognition of the economic basis of life.

But he lets us pray only for the bread that

is needful, and for that only when it becomes needful. The conception of what is needful will expand as human life develops. But this prayer can never be used to cover luxuries that debilitate, nor accumulations of property that can never be used but are sure to curse the soul of the holder with the diverse diseases of mammonism.

In this petition, too, Jesus compels us to stand together. We have to ask in common for our daily bread. We sit at the common table in God's great house, and the supply of each depends on the security of all. The more society is socialized, the clearer does that fact become, and the more just and humane its organization becomes, the more will that recognition be at the bottom of all our institutions. As we stand thus in common, looking up to God for our bread, every one of us ought to feel the sin and shame of it if he habitually takes more than his fair share and leaves others hungry that he may surfeit. It is inhuman, irreligious, and indecent.

The remaining petitions deal with the spiritual needs. Looking backward, we see that our lives have been full of sin and failure, and we realize the need of forgiveness. Looking forward, we tremble at the temptations that await us and pray for deliverance from evil.

In these prayers for the inner life, where the soul seems to confront God alone, we should expect to find only individualistic religion. But even here the social note sounds clearly.

This prayer will not permit us to ask for God's forgiveness without making us affirm that we have forgiven our brothers and are on a basis of brotherly love with all men: "Forgive us our debts, as we also have forgiven our debtors." We shall have to be socially right if we want to be religiously right. Jesus will not suffer us to be pious toward God and merciless toward men.

In the prayer, "Lead us not into temptation," we feel the human trembling of fear. Experience has taught us our frailty. Every man can see certain contingencies just a step ahead of him and knows that his moral capacity for resistance would collapse hopelessly if he were placed in these situations. Therefore Jesus gives voice to our inarticulate plea to God not to bring us into such situations.

But such situations are created largely by the social life about us. If the society in which we move is rank with sexual looseness, or full of the suggestiveness and solicitations of alcoholism; if our business life is such that we have to lie and cheat and be cruel in order to live and prosper; if our political organization offers an ambitious man the alternative of betraying the public good or of being thwarted and crippled in all his efforts, then the temptations are created in which men go under, and society frustrates the prayer we utter to God. No church can interpret this petition intelligently which closes its mind to the debasing or invigorating influence of the spiritual environment furnished by society. No man can utter this petition without conscious or unconscious hypocrisy who is helping to create the temptations in which others are sure to fall.

The words "Deliver us from the evil one" have in them the ring of battle. They bring to mind the incessant grapple between God and the permanent and malignant powers of evil in humanity. To the men of the first century that meant Satan and his host of evil spirits who ruled in the oppressive, extortionate, and idolatrous powers of Rome. Today the original spirit of that prayer will probably be best understood by those who are pitted against the terrible powers of organized covetousness and institutionalized oppression.

Thus the Lord's Prayer is the great prayer of social Christianity. It is charged with what we call "social consciousness." It assumes the social solidarity of men as a matter of course. It recognizes the social basis of all moral and religious life even in the most intimate personal relations to God.

It is not the property of those whose chief religious aim is to pass through an evil world in safety, leaving the world's evil unshaken. Its dominating thought is the moral and religious transformation of mankind in all its social relations. It was left us by Jesus, the great initiator of the Christian revolution; and it is the rightful property of those who follow his banner in the conquest of the world.

FOR MORNING, NOON, AND NIGHT

O GOD, we thank thee for the sweet refreshment of sleep and for the glory and vigor of the new day. As we set our faces once more toward our daily work, we pray thee for the strength sufficient for our tasks. May Christ's spirit of duty and service ennoble all we do. Uphold us by the consciousness that our work is useful work and a blessing to all. If there has been anything in our work harmful to others and dishonorable to ourselves, reveal it to our inner eye with such clearness that we shall hate it and put it away, though it be at a loss to ourselves. When we work with others, help us to regard them, not as servants to our will, but as brothers equal to us in human dignity, and equally worthy of their full reward. May there be nothing in this day's work of which we shall be ashamed when the sun has set, nor in the eventide of our life when our task is done and we go to our long home to meet thy face.

ONCE more a new day lies before us, our Father. As we go out among men to do our work, touching the hands and lives of our fellows, make us, we pray thee, friends of all the world. Save us from blighting the fresh flower of any heart by the flare of sudden anger or secret hate. May we not bruise the rightful self-respect of any by contempt or malice. Help us to cheer the suffering by our sympathy, to freshen the drooping by our hopefulness, and to strengthen in all the wholesome sense of worth and the joy of life. Save us from the deadly poison of class-pride. Grant that we may look all men in the face with the eyes of a brother. If any one needs us, make us ready to yield our help ungrudgingly, unless higher duties claim us, and may we rejoice that we have it in us to be helpful to our fellow-men.

O GOD, we beseech thee to save us this day from the distractions of vanity and the false lure of inordinate desires. Grant us the grace of a quiet and humble mind, and may we learn of Jesus to be meek and lowly of heart. May we not join the throng of those who seek after things that never satisfy and who draw others after them in the fever of covetousness. Save us from adding our influence to the drag of temptation. If the fierce tide of greed beats against the breakwaters of our soul, may we rest at peace in thy higher contentment. In the press of life may we pass from duty to duty in tranquillity of heart and spread thy quietness to all who come near.

O THOU great Companion of our souls, do thou go with us today and comfort us by the sense of thy presence in the hours of spiritual isolation. Give us a single eye for duty. Guide us by the voice within. May we take heed of all the judgments of men and gather patiently whatever truth they hold, but teach us still to test them by the words and the spirit of the one who alone is our Master. May we not be so wholly of one mind with the life that now is that the world can fully approve us, but may we speak the higher truth and live the purer righteousness which thou hast revealed to us. If men speak well of us, may we not be puffed up; if they slight us, may we not be cast down; remembering the words of our Master who bade us rejoice when men speak evil against us and tremble if all speak well, that so we may have evidence that we are still soldiers of God.

O GOD, we who are bound together in the tender ties of love, pray thee for a day of unclouded love. May no passing irritation rob us of our joy in one another. Forgive us if we have often been keen to see the human failings, and slow to feel the preciousness of those who are still the dearest comfort of our life. May there be no sharp words that wound and scar, and no rift that may grow into estrangement. Suffer us not to grieve those whom thou hast sent to us as the sweet ministers of love. May our eyes not be so holden by selfishness that we know thine angels only when they spread their wings to return to thee.

O LORD, we lift our hearts to thee in the pure light of morning and pray that they be kept clean of evil passion by the power of forgiving love. If any slight or wrong still rankles in our souls, help us to pluck it out and to be healed of thee. Suffer us not to turn in anger on him who has wronged us, seeking his hurt, lest we increase the sorrows of the world and taint our own souls with the poisoned sweetness of revenge. Grant that by the insight of love we may understand our brother in his wrong, and if his soul is sick, to bear with him in pity and to save him in the gentle spirit of our Master. Make us determined to love even at cost to our pride, that so we may be soldiers of thy peace on earth.

O LORD, we praise thee for our sister, the Night, who folds all the tired folk of the earth in her comfortable robe of darkness and gives them sleep. Release now the strained limbs of toil and smooth the brow of care. Grant us the refreshing draught of forgetfulness that we may rise in the morning with a smile on our face. Comfort and ease those who toss wakeful on a bed of pain, or whose aching nerves crave sleep and find it not. Save them from evil or despondent thoughts in the long darkness, and teach them so to lean on thy all-pervading life and love, that their souls may grow tranquil and their bodies, too, may rest. And now through thee we send Good Night to all our brothers and sisters near and far, and pray for peace upon all the earth.

OUR Father, as we turn to the comfort of our rest, we remember those who must wake that we may sleep. Bless the guardians of peace who protect us against men of evil will, the watchers who save us from the terrors of fire, and all the many who carry on through the hours of the night the restless commerce of men on sea and land. We thank thee for their faithfulness and sense of duty. We pray for thy pardon if our covetousness or luxury makes their nightly toil necessary. Grant that we may realize how dependent the safety of our loved ones and the comforts of our life are on these our brothers, that so we may think of them with love and gratitude and help to make their burden lighter.

ACCEPT the work of this day, O Lord, as we lay it at thy feet. Thou knowest its imperfections, and we know. Of the brave purposes of the morning only a few have found their fulfilment. We bless thee that thou art no hard taskmaster, watching grimly the stint of work we bring, but the father and teacher of men who rejoices with us as we learn to work. We have naught to boast before thee, but we do not fear thy face. Thou knowest all things and thou art love. Accept every right intention however brokenly fulfilled, but grant that ere our life is done we may under thy tuition become true master workmen, who know the art of a just and valiant life.

OUR Master, as this day closes and passes from our control, the sense of our shortcomings is quick within us and we seek thy pardon. But since we daily crave thy mercy on our weakness, help us now to show mercy to those who have this day grieved or angered us and to forgive them utterly. Suffer us not to cherish dark thoughts of resentment or revenge. So fill us with thy abounding love and peace that no ill-will may be left in our hearts as we turn to our rest. And if we remember that any brother justly hath aught against us through this day's work, fix in us this moment the firm resolve to make good the wrong and to win again the love of our brother. Suffer us not to darken thy world by lovelessness, but give us the power of the sons of God to bring in the reign of love among men.

OUR Father, we thank thee for all the friendly folk who have come into our life this day, gladdening us by their human kindness, and we send them now our parting thoughts of love through thee. We bless thee that we are set amidst this rich brotherhood of kindred life with its mysterious power to quicken and uplift. Make us eager to pay the due price for what we get by putting forth our own life in wholesome good will and by bearing cheerily the troubles that go with all joys. Above all we thank thee for those who share our higher life, the comrades of our better self, in whose companionship we break the mystic bread of life and feel the glow of thy wonderful presence. Into thy keeping we commit our friends, and pray that we may never lose their love by losing thee.

O GOD, in whom is neither near nor far, through thee we yearn for those who belong to us and who are not here with us. We would fain be near them to shield them from harm and to touch them with the tenderness of love. We cast our cares for them on thee in this evening hour, and pray thee to do better for them than we could do. May no distance have power to wean their hearts from us and no sloth of ours cause us to lag behind the even pace of growth. In due time restore them to us and gladden our souls with their sweet sight. We remember too the loved ones into whose dear eyes we cannot look again. O God, in whom are both the living and the dead, thou art still their life and light as thou art ours. Wherever they be, lay thy hand tenderly upon them and grant that some day we may meet again and hear once more their broken words of love.

PRAYER FOR SUNDAY MORNING

O GOD, we rejoice that today no burden of work will be upon us and that our body and soul are free to rest. We thank thee that of old this day was hallowed by thee for all who toil, and that from generation to generation the weary sons of men have found it a shelter and a breathing space. We pray for thy peace on all our brothers and sisters who are glad to cease from labor and to enjoy the comfort of their home and the companionship of those whom they love. Forbid that the pressure of covetousness or thoughtless love of pleasure rob any who are worn of their divine right of rest. Grant us wisdom and self-control that our pleasures may not be follies, lest our leisure drain us more than our work. Teach us that in the mystic unity of our nature our body cannot rest unless our soul has repose, that so we may walk this day in thy presence in tranquillity of spirit, taking each joy as thy gift, and on the morrow return to our labor refreshed and content.

PRAYER FOR SUNDAY EVENING

O LORD, we lift our souls to thee in the awe of the eventide. Above the tree-tops hang the heavens in their glory, but above the stars art thou and the eternal silence. We rejoice that in the quiet of thy day of rest our spirits have been attuned to the melodies of thy beauty. We bless thee for every word of solemn truth which has entered our hearts, for every touch of loving hand that has comforted us, for every opportunity we have had to speak some message from our heart to the heart of our brothers. Forgive us if any hours have been wasted on profitless things that have brought us no satisfaction, or if we have dragged our dusty cares into thy sacred day and made the holy common. We pray for thy blessing on all who have come near to us this day, on all who have brought us strength, on all who are sad and hungry for thee, on all thy great humanity in its sin and beauty. May our last waking thought be a benediction for our fellows and in our sleep may we still be with thee.

GRACE BEFORE MEAT

OUR Father, thou art the final source of all our comforts and to thee we render thanks for this food. But we also remember in gratitude the many men and women whose labor was necessary to produce it, and who gathered it from the land and afar from the sea for our sustenance. Grant that they too may enjoy the fruit of their labor without want, and may be bound up with us in a fellowship of thankful hearts.

O GOD, we thank thee for the abundance of our blessings, but we pray that our plenty may not involve want for others. Do thou satisfy the desire of every child of thine. Grant that the strength which we shall draw from this food may be put forth again for the common good, and that our life may return to humanity a full equivalent in useful work for the nourishment which we receive from the common store.

OUR Father, we thank thee for the food of our body, and for the human love which is the food of our hearts. Bless our family circle, and make this meal a sacrament of love to all who are gathered at this table. But bless thou too that great family of humanity of which we are but a little part. Give to all thy children their daily bread, and let our family not enjoy its comforts in selfish isolation.

O LORD, we pray for thy presence at this meal. Hallow all our joys, and if there is anything wanton or unholy in them, open our eyes that we may see. If we have ever gained our bread by injustice, or eaten it in heartlessness, cleanse our life and give us a spirit of humility and love, that we may be worthy to sit at the common table of humanity in the great house of our Father.

BEFORE A PARTING

O GOD, as we break bread once more before we part, we turn to thee with the burden of our desires. Go with him who leaves us and hold him safe. May he feel that we shall not forget him and that his place can never be filled till he returns. Make this meal a sacrament of human love to us, and may our hearts divine the thoughts too tender to be spoken.

FOR A FAMILY REUNION

O LORD, our hearts are full of gratitude and praise, for after the long days of separation thou hast brought us together again to look into the dear faces and read their love as of old. As the happy memories of the years when we were young together rise up to cheer us, may we feel anew how closely our lives were wrought into one another in their early making, and what a treasure we have had in our home. Whatever new friendships we may form, grant that the old loves may abide to the end and grow ever sweeter with the ripening years.

FOR A GUEST

OUR Father, we rejoice in the guest who sits at meat with us, for our food is the more welcome because he shares it, and our home the dearer because it shelters him. Grant that in the happy exchange of thought and affection we may realize anew that all our gladness comes from the simple fellowship of our human kind, and that we are rich as long as we are loved.

IN TIME OF TROUBLE

O LORD, thou knowest that we are sore stricken and heavy of heart. We beseech thee to uphold us by thy comfort. Thou wert the God of our fathers, and in all these years thine arm has never failed us, for our strength has ever been as our days. May this food come to us as an assurance of thy love and care and a promise of thy sustenance and relief.

PRAISE AND THANKSGIVING

FOR THE FATHERHOOD OF GOD

O THOU great Father of us all, we rejoice that at last we know thee. All our soul within us is glad because we need no longer cringe before thee as slaves of holy fear, seeking to appease thine anger by sacrifice and self-inflicted pain, but may come like little children, trustful and happy, to the God of love. Thou art the only true father, and all the tender beauty of our human loves is the reflected radiance of thy loving kindness, like the moonlight from the sunlight, and testifies to the eternal passion that kindled it.

Grant us growth of spiritual vision, that with the passing years we may enter into the fulness of this our faith. Since thou art our Father, may we not hide our sins from thee, but overcome them by the stern comfort of thy presence. By this knowledge uphold us in our sorrows and make us patient even amid the unsolved mysteries of the years. Reveal to us the larger goodness and love that speak through the unbending laws of thy world. Through this faith make us the willing equals of all thy other children.

As thou art ever pouring out thy life in sacrificial father-love, may we accept the eternal law of the cross and give ourselves to thee and to all men. We praise thee for Jesus Christ, whose life has revealed to us this faith and law, and we rejoice that he has become the first-born among many brethren. Grant that in us, too, the faith in thy fatherhood may shine through all our life with such persuasive beauty that some who still creep in the dusk of fear may stand erect as free sons of God, and that others who now through unbelief are living as orphans in an empty world may stretch out their hands to the great Father of their spirits and find thee near.

FOR THIS WORLD

O GOD, we thank thee for this universe, our great home; for its vastness and its riches, and for the manifoldness of the life which teems upon it and of which we are part. We praise thee for the arching sky and the blessed winds, for the driving clouds and the constellations on high. We praise thee for the salt sea and the running water, for the everlasting hills, for the trees, and for the grass under our feet. We thank thee for our senses by which we can see the splendor of the morning, and hear the jubilant songs of love, and smell the breath of the springtime. Grant us, we pray thee, a heart wide open to all this joy and beauty, and save our souls from being so steeped in care or so darkened by passion that we pass heedless and unseeing when even the thorn-bush by the wayside is aflame with the glory of God.

Enlarge within us the sense of fellowship with all the living things, our little brothers, to whom thou hast given this earth as their home in common with us. We remember with shame that in the past we have exercised the high dominion of man with ruthless cruelty, so that the voice of the Earth, which should have gone up to thee in song, has been a groan of travail. May we realize that they live, not for us alone, but for themselves and for thee, and that they love the sweetness of life even as we, and serve thee in their place better than we in ours.

When our use of this world is over and we make room for others, may we not leave anything ravished by our greed or spoiled by our ignorance, but may we hand on our common heritage fairer and sweeter through our use of it, undiminished in fertility and joy, that so our bodies may return in peace to the great mother who nourished them and our spirits may round the circle of a perfect life in thee.

FOR SOCIAL GROUPS AND CLASSES

FOR CHILDREN WHO WORK

O THOU great Father of the weak, lay thy hand tenderly on all the little children on earth and bless them. Bless our own children, who are life of our life, and who have become the heart of our heart. Bless every little child-friend that has leaned against our knee and refreshed our soul by its smiling trustfulness. Be good to all children who long in vain for human love, or for flowers and water, and the sweet breast of Nature. But bless with a sevenfold blessing the young lives whose slender shoulders are already bowed beneath the yoke of toil, and whose glad growth is being stunted forever. Suffer not their little bodies to be utterly sapped, and their minds to be given over to stupidity and the vices of an empty soul. We have all jointly deserved the millstone of thy wrath for making these little ones to stumble and fall. Grant all employers of labor stout hearts to refuse enrichment at such a price. Grant to all the citizens and officers of states which now permit this wrong the grace of holy anger. Help us to realize that every child of our nation is in very truth our child, a member of our great family. By the Holy Child that nestled in Mary's bosom; by the memories of our own childhood joys and sorrows; by the sacred possibilities that slumber in every child, we beseech thee to save us from killing the sweetness of young life by the greed of gain.

FOR THE CHILDREN OF THE STREET

O HEAVENLY Father, whose unveiled face the angels of little children do always behold, look with love and pity, we beseech thee, upon the children of the streets. Where men, in their busy and careless lives, have made a highway, these children of thine have made a home and a school, and are learning the bad lessons of our selfishness and our folly. Save them, and save us, O Lord. Save them from ignorance and brutality, from the shamelessness of lust, the hardness of greed, and the besotting of drink; and save us from the greater guilt of those that offend thy little ones, and from the hypocrisy of those that say they see and see not, whose sin remaineth.

Make clear to those of older years the inalienable right of childhood to play, and give to those who govern our cities the will and ability to provide the places for play; make clear to those who minister to the appetite for recreation the guilt of them that lead astray thy children; and make clear to us all that the great school of life is not encompassed by walls and that its teachers are all who influence their younger brethren by companionship and example, whether for good or evil, and that in that school all we are teachers and as we teach are judged. For all false teaching, for all hindering of thy children, pardon us, O Lord, and suffer the little children to come unto thee, for Jesus' sake.

MORNAY WILLIAMS.

FOR WOMEN WHO TOIL

O GOD, we pray thee for our sisters who are leaving the ancient shelter of the home to earn their wage in the factory and the store amid the press of modern life. Save them from the strain of unremitting toil that would unfit them for the holy duties of home and motherhood which the future may lay upon them. Give them grace to cherish under the new surroundings the old sweetness and gentleness of womanhood, and in the rough mingling of life to keep their hearts pure and their lives untarnished. Save them from the terrors of utter want. Teach them to stand loyally by their sisters, that by united action they may better their common lot.

If it must be so that our women toil like men, help us still to reverence in them the mothers of the future. But make us determined to shield them from unequal burdens, that the women of our nation be not drained of strength and hope for the enrichment of a few, lest our homes grow poor in the wifely sweetness and motherly love which have been the saving strength and glory of our country. To such as yearn for the love and sovereign freedom of their own home, grant in due time the fulfilment of their sweet desires. By Mary, the beloved, who bore the world's redemption in her bosom; by the memory of our own dear mothers who kissed our souls awake; by the little daughters who must soon go out into that world which we are now fashioning for others, we beseech thee that we may deal aright by all women.

FOR WORKINGMEN

O GOD, thou mightiest worker of the universe, source of all strength and author of all unity, we pray thee for our brothers, the industrial workers of the nation. As their work binds them together in common toil and danger, may their hearts be knit together in a strong sense of their common interests and destiny. Help them to realize that the injury of one is the concern of all, and that the welfare of all must be the aim of every one. If any of them is tempted to sell the birthright of his class for a mess of pottage for himself, give him a wider outlook and a nobler sympathy with his fellows. Teach them to keep step in a steady onward march, and in their own way to fulfil the law of Christ by bearing the common burdens.

Grant the organizations of labor quiet patience and prudence in all disputes, and fairness to see the other side. Save them from malice and bitterness. Save them from the headlong folly which ruins a fair cause, and give them wisdom resolutely to put aside the two-edged sword of violence that turns on those who seize it. Raise up for them still more leaders of able mind and large heart, and give them grace to follow the wiser counsel.

When they strive for leisure and health and a better wage, do thou grant their cause success, but teach them not to waste their gain on fleeting passions, but to use it in building fairer homes and a nobler manhood. Grant all classes of our nation a larger comprehension for the aspirations of labor and for the courage and worth of these our brothers, that we may cheer them in their struggles and understand them even in their sins. And may the upward climb of Labor, its defeats and its victories, in the farther reaches bless all classes of our nation, and build up for the republic of the future a great body of workers, strong of limb, clear of mind, fair in temper, glad to labor, conscious of their worth, and striving together for the final brotherhood of all men.

FOR IMMIGRANTS

O THOU great Champion of the outcast and the weak, we remember before thee the people of other nations who are coming to our land, seeking bread, a home, and a future. May we look with thy compassion upon those who have been drained and stunted by the poverty and oppression of centuries, and whose minds have been warped by superstition or seared by the dumb agony of revolt. We bless thee for all that America has meant to the alien folk that have crossed the sea in the past, and for all the patient strength and God-fearing courage with which they have enriched our nation. We rejoice in the millions whose life has expanded in the wealth and liberty of our country, and whose children have grown to fairer stature and larger thoughts; for we, too, are the children of immigrants, who came with anxious hearts and halting feet on the westward path of hope.

We beseech thee that our republic may no longer fail their trust. We mourn for the dark sins of past and present, wherein men who are held in honor among us made spoil of the ignorance and helplessness of the strangers and sent them to an early death. In a nation dedicated to liberty may they not find the old oppression and a fiercer greed. May they never find that the arm of the law is but the arm of the strong. Help our whole people henceforth to keep in leash the cunning that would devour the simple. May they feel here the pure air of freedom and face the morning radiance of a joyous hope.

For all the oppressed afar off who sigh for liberty; for all lovers of the people who strive to break their shackles; for all who dare to believe in democracy and the kingdom of God, make thou our great commonwealth once more a sure beacon-light of hope and a guide on the path which leads to the perfect union of law and liberty.

FOR EMPLOYERS

WE invoke thy grace and wisdom, O Lord, upon all men of good will who employ and control the labor of men. Amid the numberless irritations and anxieties of their position, help them to keep a quiet and patient temper, and to rule firmly and wisely, without harshness and anger. Since they hold power over the bread, the safety, and the hopes of the workers, may they wield their powers justly and with love, as older brothers and leaders in the great fellowship of labor. Suffer not the heavenly light of compassion for the weak and the old to be quenched in their hearts. When they are tempted to follow the ruthless ways of others, and to sacrifice human health and life for profit, do thou strengthen their will in the hour of need, and bring to naught the counsels of the heartless. Save them from repressing their workers into sullen submission and helpless fear. May they not sin against the Christ by using the bodies and souls of men as mere tools to make things, forgetting the human hearts and longings of these their brothers.

Raise up among us employers who shall be makers of men as well as of goods. Give us masters of industry who will use their higher ability and knowledge in lifting the workers to increasing independence and vigor, and who will train their helpers for the larger responsibilities of the coming age. Give us men of faith who will see beyond the strife of the present and catch a vision of a nobler organization of our work, when all will still follow the leadership of the ablest, not in fear but by the glad will of all, and when none shall be master and none shall be man, but all shall stand side by side in a strong and righteous brotherhood of work.

FOR MEN IN BUSINESS

WE plead with thee, O God, for our brothers who are pressed by the cares and beset by the temptations of business life. We acknowledge before thee our common guilt for the hardness and deceitfulness of industry and trade which lead us all into temptation and cause even the righteous to slip and fall. As long as man is set against man in a struggle for wealth, help the men in business to make their contest, as far as may be, a test of excellence, by which even the defeated may be spurred to better work. If any man is pitted against those who have forgotten fairness and honesty, help him to put his trust resolutely in the profitableness of sincerity and uprightness, and, if need be, to accept loss rather than follow on crooked paths.

Establish in unshaken fidelity all who hold in trust the savings of others. Since the wealth and welfare of our nation are controlled by our business men, cause them to realize that they serve not themselves alone, but hold high public functions, and do thou save them from betraying the interests of the many for their own enrichment, lest a new tyranny grow up in a land that is dedicated to freedom. Grant them far-sighted patriotism to subordinate their profits to the public weal, and a steadfast determination to transform the disorder of the present into the nobler and freer harmony of the future. May thy Spirit, O God, which is ceaselessly pleading within us, prevail at last to bring our business life under Christ's law of service, so that all who share in the processes of factory and trade may grow up into that high consciousness of a divine calling which blesses those who are the free servants of God and the people and who consciously devote their strength to the common good.

FOR CONSUMERS

O GOD, thou Father of us all, we praise thee that thou hast bound humanity in a great unity of life so that each must lean on the strength of all, and depend for his comfort and safety on the help and labor of his brothers.

We invoke thy blessing on all the men and women who have toiled to build and warm our homes, to fashion our raiment, and to wrest from sea and land the food that nourishes us and our children.

We pray that they may have health and joy, and hope and love, even as we desire for our own loved ones.

Grant us wisdom to deal justly and fraternally with every man and woman whom we face in the business of life.

May we not unknowingly inflict suffering through selfish indifference or the wilful ignorance of a callous heart.

Since the comforts of our life are brought to us from afar, and made by those whom we

First Published by "THE SURVEY." Used by permission.

do not know nor see, grant us organized intelligence and power that we may send the command of our righteous will along the channels of trade and industry, and help to cleanse them of hardness and unfairness.

May the time come when we need wear and use nothing that is wet in thy sight with human tears, or cheapened by wearing down the lives of the weak.

Save us, we beseech thee, from unconscious guilt.

Speak thou to our souls and bid us strive for the coming of thy kingdom of justice when thy merciful and saving will shall be done on earth.

FOR KINGS AND MAGNATES

O GOD, we worship thee as the sole lord and sovereign of humanity, and render free obedience to thee because thy laws are just and thy will is love. We pray thee for the kings and princes of the nations to whom power has descended from the past, and for the lords of industry and trade in whose hands the wealth and power of our modern world have gathered. We beseech thee to save them from the terrible temptations of their position, lest they follow in the somber lineage of those who have lorded it in the past and have used the people's powers for their oppression. Suffer them not to waste the labor of the many for their own luxury, or to use the precious life-blood of men for the corruption of all. Open their hearts to the saving spirit of the new age of freedom. Mature in their souls the unshakeable conviction that all they have is but held in trust for a time till the heir shall claim his own.

And when the people seek the ampler freedom and self-direction of manhood, may there be no blindness to the higher will and no hardening of heart by those who have ruled. Grant them wisdom so large-hearted that they may recognize the culmination of their task in yielding up their powers, and may use their gathered knowledge in guiding the liberation of the people in order and stability. Save them from the fear and hate which are the tyrants' portion and from the scorn of coming generations. Reveal to them that all the higher joys come only by imparting the strength of our life to those who need it, and that a man's life consisteth not in the things which he possesses, but in the love that flows out from him and flows back to him.

FOR DISCOVERERS AND INVENTORS

WE praise thee, O Lord, for that mysterious spark of thy light within us, the intellect of man, for thou hast kindled it in the beginning and by the breath of thy spirit it has grown to flaming power in our race.

We rejoice in the men of genius and intellectual vision who discern the undiscovered applications of thy laws and dig the deeper springs through which the hidden forces of thy world may well up to the light of day. We claim them as our own in thee, as members with us in the common body of humanity, of which thou art the all-pervading life and inspirer. Grant them, we pray thee, the divine humility of thine elect souls, to realize that they are sent of thee as brothers and helpers of men and that the powers within them are but part of the vast equipment of humanity, entrusted to them for the common use. May they bow to the law of Christ and live, not to be served, but to give their abilities for the emancipation of the higher life of man. Save them from turning thy revelations into means of extortion and from checking the toilsome march of humanity till they take toll.

But to us who benefit by their work do thou grant wisdom and justice that we may not suffer the fruit of their toil to be wrested from them by selfish cunning or the pressure of need, but may assure them of their fair reward and of the meed of love and honor that is the due of those who have served humanity well. Gladden us by the glowing consciousness of the one life that thinks and strives in us all, and knit us together into a commonwealth of brothers in which each shall be heir of all things and the free servant of all men.

FOR ARTISTS AND MUSICIANS

O THOU who art the all-pervading glory of the world, we bless thee for the power of beauty to gladden our hearts. We praise thee that even the least of us may feel a thrill of thy creative joy when we give form and substance to our thoughts and, beholding our handiwork, find it good and fair.

We praise thee for our brothers, the masters of form and color and sound, who have power to unlock for us the vaster spaces of emotion and to lead us by their hand into the reaches of nobler passions. We rejoice in their gifts and pray thee to save them from the temptations which beset their powers. Save them from the discouragements of a selfish ambition and from the vanity that feeds on cheap applause, from the snare of the senses and from the dark phantoms that haunt the listening soul.

Let them not satisfy their hunger for beauty with tricks of skill, turning the art of God into a petty craft of men. Teach them that they, too, are but servants of humanity, and that the promise of their gifts can fulfil itself only in the service of love. Give them faith in the inspiring power of a great purpose and courage to follow to the end the visions of their youth. Kindle in their hearts a passionate pity for the joyless lives of the people, and make them rejoice if they are found worthy to hold the cup of beauty to lips that are athirst. Make them the reverent interpreters of God to man, who see thy face and hear thy voice in all things, that so they may unveil for us the beauties of nature which we have passed unseeing, and the sadness and sweetness of humanity to which our selfishness has made us blind.

FOR JUDGES

O GOD, who art the author and giver of law, from whom alone all just designs and righteous judgments proceed, give unto all those who frame, interpret, or administer human law the counsel of thy Holy Spirit, that they may know themselves thy ministers. Remove from them all pride and vainglory of class, all prejudice of birth and training, all narrowness of place and power, and grant them to know that only in loving sympathy with all their fellow men is there the possibility of clear understanding and righteous decision. Enable them so to receive the precepts and examples of the past that they build upon the heritage of the fathers a just and adequate edifice of law for the present.

As they deduce the principles which underlie the customary laws of men, give unto them the larger vision of the reign of law and the ordered universe, of the precedents of nature and providence, and suffer them not to forget or to be ignorant of those inevitable laws of thine which outlive the lives of men. O Thou who hast given to man the will to conquer the earth, the power to serve his fellows and the heart to love thee, may the rule of the market-place never be suffered to obscure thine eternal justice, but grant to all these the ministers of human justice the will and ability to pacify the passions and adjust the disputes of men. Suffer them neither to be swayed by the prejudices nor to appeal to the weaknesses of others, but to deal fairly, counsel wisely, and quit themselves manfully in all matters; to be the servants of all men, but the hirelings of none, and so to hasten the coming of the kingdom of God on earth, for which we pray.

MORNAY WILLIAMS.

FOR LAWYERS AND LEGISLATORS

O LORD, thou art the eternal order of the universe. Our human laws at best are but an approximation to thine immutable law, and if our institutions are to stand, they must rest on justice, for only justice can endure. We beseech thee for the men who are set to make and interpret the laws of our nation. Grant to all lawyers a deep consciousness that they are called of God to see justice done, and that they prostitute a holy duty if ever they connive in its defeat. Fill them with a high determination to make the courts of our land a strong fortress of defense for the poor and weak, and never a castle of oppression for the hard and cunning.

Save them from surrendering the dear-bought safeguards of the people for which our fathers fought and suffered. Revive in them the spirit of the great liberators of the past that they may cleanse our law of the inherited wrongs that still cling to it.

Suffer not the web of outgrown precedents to veil their moral vision, but grant them a penetrating eye for the rights and wrongs of today and a quick human sympathy with the life and sufferings of the people. May they not perpetuate the tangles of the law for the profit of their profession. Aid them to make its course so simple, and its justice so swift and sure, that the humblest may safely trust it and the strongest fear it. Grant them wisdom so to refashion all law that it may become the true expression of the fairer ideals of freedom and brotherhood which are now seeking their incarnation in a new age. Make these our brothers the wise interpreters of thine eternal law, the brave spokesmen of thy will, and in reward bestow upon them the joy of conscious fellowship with thy Christ in saving men from the bondage of ancient wrong.

FOR USE IN PRISONS AND JAILS

O GOD, we men and women in prison make our prayer to thee. We too claim thee as the Father of our spirit and the great Friend of our better self.

Men have passed judgment on us by our outward acts, but thou alone knowest all things. Thou knowest how some of us were burdened by the sins of our ancestors; and some were tainted with vice in our youth before we understood; and some made a brave fight, but the powers of evil were strong; and some thought they were doing right when they broke the law. We would hide nothing from thee, O thou Searcher of Hearts, but we pray thee to pardon the frailties and mistakes of the past, and in the years still left to us do thou build up our lives to noble manhood and womanhood.

Give us back our freedom in due time. Protect our dear ones while we are away, and grant that soon we may once more hold them in our arms and read their love and forgiveness in their sweet faces.

Make a place for us where we can do honest and wholesome work among our fellow men. Give us strength to maintain our honor and never again to give needless sorrow to those who love us.

We pray thee for patience and hopefulness in these long and lonely days. May no unclean or hateful thoughts gain the mastery over our souls. May we be friends with all men of good will, and if any wrong us, may we have the spirit of Jesus Christ, who also was a prisoner and who prayed for those that hurt him.

May all the great world of men be filled more and more with thy saving love, so that fewer men and women may be snared in temptation, and those who go wrong may be turned back to the right without the need of prisons. Grant that our own experience may in some way help others, that so our life may not be lived in vain, but may add a little to the common good and joy of mankind in the better days to come.

FOR PUBLIC OFFICERS

O GOD, thou great governor of all the world, we pray thee for all who hold public office and power, for the life, the welfare, and the virtue of the people are in their hands to make or to mar. We remember with shame that in the past the mighty have preyed on the labors of the poor; that they have laid nations in the dust by their oppression, and have thwarted the love and the prayers of thy servants. We bless thee that the new spirit of democracy has touched even the kings of the earth. We rejoice that by the free institutions of our country the tyrannous instincts of the strong may be curbed and turned to the patient service of the commonwealth.

Strengthen the sense of duty in our political life. Grant that the servants of the state may feel ever more deeply that any diversion of their public powers for private ends is a betrayal of their country. Purge our cities and states and nation of the deep causes of corruption which have so often made sin profitable and uprightness hard. Bring to an end the stale days of party cunning. Breathe a new spirit into all our nation. Lift us from the dust and mire of the past that we may gird ourselves for a new day's work. Give our leaders a new vision of the possible future of our country and set their hearts on fire with large resolves. Raise up a new generation of public men, who will have the faith and daring of the kingdom of God in their hearts, and who will enlist for life in a holy warfare for the freedom and rights of the people.

FOR DOCTORS AND NURSES

WE praise thee, O God, for our friends, the doctors and nurses, who seek the healing of our bodies. We bless thee for their gentleness and patience, for their knowledge and skill. We remember the hours of our suffering when they brought relief, and the days of our fear and anguish at the bedside of our dear ones when they came as ministers of God to save the life thou hadst given. May we reward their fidelity and devotion by our loving gratitude, and do thou uphold them by the satisfaction of work well done.

We rejoice in the tireless daring with which some are now tracking the great slayers of mankind by the white light of science. Grant that under their teaching we may grapple with the sins which have ever dealt death to the race, and that we may so order the life of our communities that none may be doomed to an untimely death for lack of the simple gifts which thou hast given in abundance. Make thou our doctors the prophets and soldiers of thy kingdom, which is the reign of cleanliness and self-restraint and the dominion of health and joyous life.

Strengthen in their whole profession the consciousness that their calling is holy and that they, too, are disciples of the saving Christ. May they never through the pressure of need or ambition surrender the sense of a divine mission and become hirelings who serve only for money. Make them doubly faithful in the service of the poor who need their help most sorely, and may the children of the workingman be as precious to them as the child of the rich. Though they deal with the frail body of man, may they have an abiding sense of the eternal value of the life residing in it, that by the call of faith and hope they may summon to their aid the mysterious spirit of man and the powers of thy all-pervading life.

A TUBERCULOSIS DAY PRAYER

O GOD, we pray thee for all whose vigor is being drained by slow and wasting illness. Strengthen their powers as they battle for their life, and if it be possible, we beseech thee to restore them and grant them the fulness of their years. If their strength is failing, give them courage still to labor cheerfully and to leave to those who love them dear memories of faith and patience for the distant days.

Since we are all jointly guilty of the conditions which have bred their disease, may we stand by those who bear the burden of our common sin, and set the united will of our community against this power that slays the young and strong in the bloom of their life. May this death that creeps from man to man be a solemn reminder that we are all one family, bound together in joy and sorrow, in life and death, that we may cease from our selfish indifference and together seek thy kingdom and thy righteousness which will bring us health and life.

First Published by "THE SURVEY." Used by permission.

FOR WRITERS AND NEWSPAPER MEN

O THOU great source of truth and knowledge, we remember before thee all whose calling it is to gather and winnow the facts for informing the people. Inspire them with a determined love for honest work and a stanch hatred for the making of lies, lest the judgments of our nation be perverted and we be taught to call light darkness and darkness light. Since the sanity and wisdom of a nation are in their charge, may they count it shame to set the baser passions of men on fire for the sake of gain. May they never suffer themselves to be used in drugging the mind of the people with falsehood and prejudice.

Grant them boldness to turn the unwelcome light on those who love the darkness because their deeds are evil. Put into their hands the shining sword of truth, and make them worthy successors of the great champions of the people who held truth to be a holy thing by which nations live and for which men should die. Cause them to realize that they have a public function in the commonwealth, and that their country may be saved by their courage or undone by their cowardice and silence. Grant them the heart of manhood to cast their mighty influence with the forces that make the people strong and free, and if they suffer loss, may they rejoice in that as proof to their own souls that they have fought a good fight and have been servants of the higher law.

FOR MINISTERS

O JESUS, we thy ministers bow before thee to confess the common sins of our calling. Thou knowest all things; thou knowest that we love thee and that our hearts' desire is to serve thee in faithfulness; and yet, like Peter, we have so often failed thee in the hour of thy need. If ever we have loved our own leadership and power when we sought to lead our people to thee, we pray thee to forgive. If we have been engrossed in narrow duties and little questions, when the vast needs of humanity called aloud for prophetic vision and apostolic sympathy, we pray thee to forgive. If in our loyalty to the Church of the past we have distrusted thy living voice and have suffered thee to pass from our door unheard, we pray thee to forgive. If ever we have been more concerned for the strong and the rich than for the shepherdless throngs of the people for whom thy soul grieved, we pray thee to forgive.

O Master, amidst our failures we cast ourselves upon thee in humility and contrition. We need new light and a new message. We need the ancient spirit of prophecy and the leaping fire and joy of a new conviction, and thou alone canst give it. Inspire the ministry of thy Church with dauntless courage to face the vast needs of the future. Free us from all entanglements that have hushed our voice and bound our action. Grant us grace to look upon the veiled sins of the rich and the coarse vices of the poor through thine eyes. Give us thine inflexible sternness against sin, and thine inexhaustible compassion for the frailty and tragedy of those who do the sin. Make us faithful shepherds of thy flock, true seers of God, and true followers of Jesus.

FOR TEACHERS

WE implore thy blessing, O God, on all the men and women who teach the children and youth of our nation, for they are the potent friends and helpers of our homes. Into their hands we daily commit the dearest that we have, and as they make our children, so shall future years see them. Grant them an abiding consciousness that they are co-workers with thee, thou great teacher of humanity, and that thou hast charged them with the holy duty of bringing forth from the budding life of the young the mysterious stores of character and ability which thou hast hidden in them. Teach them to reverence the young lives, clean and plastic, which have newly come from thee, and to realize that generations still unborn shall rue their sloth or rise to higher levels through their wisdom and faithfulness. Gird them for their task with thy patience and tranquillity, with a great fatherly and motherly love for the young, and with special tenderness for the backward and afflicted. Save them from physical exhaustion, from loneliness and discouragement, from the numbness of routine, and from all bitterness of heart.

We bless thee for the free and noble spirit that is breathing with quickening power upon the educational life of our day, and for the men and women of large mind and loving heart who have made that spirit our common possession by their teaching and example. But grant that a higher obedience and self-restraint may grow in the new atmosphere of freedom. We remember with gratitude to thee the godly teachers of our own youth who won our hearts to higher purposes by the sacred contagion of their life. May the strength and beauty of Christlike service still be plainly wrought in the lives of their successors, that our children may not want for strong models of devout manhood on whom their characters can be molded.

Do thou reward thy servants with a glad sense of their own eternal worth as teachers of the race, and in the heat of the day do thou show them the spring by the wayside that flows from the eternal silence of God and gives new light to the eyes of all who drink of it.

FOR USE IN BOYS' SCHOOLS

OUR Father, we thank thee for this day, for its work and its pleasures, for the zest of our youth and the joy of living. May no mean word or foul act cloud our satisfaction or humble our pride when this day is done.

Grant that we may do our day's work with a willing heart, looking forward to the larger tasks of our life in the days to come, and may we go to meet the future years with a trained body and mind, well able to do a man's work.

May no idleness or love of easy ways, no hidden vice or flaw of character weaken our youth, lest when we strain to run the race of life, we be forced to drop out before the goal is reached.

Make us loyal to our friends, our teammates, our school and our teachers, and lovingly loyal to our parents and the dear folks at home. Save us from bringing to shame the hope and pride with which they think of us.

Give us a brave heart to say what is true and do what is right, even to our own hurt, following in the footsteps of the great Captain of our life, Jesus Christ, in whose name we make our prayer.

FOR ALL MOTHERS

O GOD, we offer thee praise and benediction for the sweet ministries of motherhood in human life. We bless thee for our own dear mothers who built up our lives by theirs; who bore us in travail and loved us the more for the pain we gave; who nourished us at their breast and hushed us to sleep in the warm security of their arms. We thank thee for their tireless love, for their voiceless prayers, for the agony with which they followed us through our sins and won us back, for the Christly power of sacrifice and redemption in mother-love. We pray thee to forgive us if in thoughtless selfishness we have taken their love as our due without giving the tenderness which they craved as their sole reward. And if the great treasure of a mother's life is still spared to us, may we do for her feebleness what she did for ours.

We remember before thee all the good women who are now bearing the pain and weariness of maternity. Grant them strength of body and mind for their new tasks. Widen their vision that they may see themselves, not as the mothers of one child alone, but as the patriot women of their nation, who alone can build up the better future with fresh and purer life. Put upon the girls of our people the awe of their future calling, that they may preserve their bodies and minds in purity and strength for the holy task to which the future may summon them.

Bestow thy special grace, we beseech thee, on all women who have the yearnings of motherhold, but whose lives are barren of its joys. If any form of human sin has robbed them of the prize of life, grant them righteous anger and valiant hearts to fight that sin on behalf of those who come after them. Help them to overcome the bitterness of disappointment, and to find an outlet for their thwarted mother-love in the wider ministrations to all the lonely and unmothered hearts in thy great family on earth.

As the protecting love of motherhood wrought blindly in the earliest upward climb of life, may it now, with open eyes and strong with Christly passion, set its tireless strength to lift humanity from the reign of brutal force and to found the larger family of men on the blessed might of love.

FOR ALL TRUE LOVERS

WE invoke thy gentlest blessings, our Father, on all true lovers. We praise thee for the great longing that draws the soul of man and maid together and bids them leave all the dear bonds of the past to cleave to one another. We thank thee for the revealing power of love which divines in the one beloved the mystic beauty and glory of humanity. We thank thee for the transfiguring power of love which ripens and ennobles our nature, calling forth the hidden stores of tenderness and strength and overcoming the selfishness of youth by the passion of self-surrender.

We pray thee to make their love strong, holy, and deathless, that no misunderstandings may fray the bond, and no gray disenchantment of the years may have power to quench the heavenly light that now glows in them. May they early gain wisdom to discern the true values of life, and may no tyranny of fashion and no glamour of cheaper joys filch from them the wholesome peace and inward satisfaction which only loyal love can give.

Grant them with sober eyes to look beyond these sweet days of friendship to the generations yet to come, and to realize that the home for which they long will be part of the sacred tissue of the body of humanity in which thou art to dwell, that so they may reverence themselves and drink the cup of joy with awe.

FOR THE BABIES

Written for the Milk and Baby Hygiene Association of Boston

O GOD, since thou hast laid the little children into our arms in utter helplessness, with no protection save our love, we pray that the sweet appeal of their baby hands may not be in vain. Let no innocent life in our city be quenched again in useless pain through our ignorance and sin. May we who are mothers or fathers seek eagerly to join wisdom to our love, lest love itself be deadly when unguided by knowledge. Bless the doctors and nurses, and all the friends of men, who are giving of their skill and devotion to the care of our children. If there are any who were kissed by love in their own infancy, but who have no child to whom they may give as they have received, grant them such largeness of sympathy that they may rejoice to pay their debt in full to all children who have need of them.

First Published by "THE SURVEY." Used by permission.

Forgive us, our Father, for the heartlessness of the past. Grant us great tenderness for all babes who suffer, and a growing sense of the divine mystery that is brooding in the soul of every child.

FOR USE BY WOMEN'S ASSOCIATIONS

O GOD, we thank thee for the human loves that are so dear to us. Bless, we beseech thee, all who are bound to us by the strong bonds of blood, of comradeship, and of love, and may none whom we have ever held dear, slip away from our heart and memory. Be with those who are far from us, and speak to their hearts the comforting words that we would love to say.

Our thoughts go out, too, beyond the closer circle of our friends to the great fellowship of human life of which we are part. Grant us to realize that in our sins and our sorrows, in our prosperity and our redemption, we are all members of one great family. Bless especially our sisters who toil for their wage, and who bear the burden of ceaseless work and frequent weariness. Give them strength of body and courage of heart. Supply them with their daily bread and all needed comfort. Teach them to stand by one another in loyalty

Used by permission of "THE WOMAN'S PRESS."

to better their common lot, and patiently to fulfil the law of Christ by bearing one another's burdens. May they still feel the mysterious presence of the Master in the rush of life, and be filled with the strength and serenity of the children of God, that so thy peace may flow out from them, and touch other restless and despairing hearts with new health of soul, through Jesus Christ, our Lord.

FOR A BIG SISTER CLUB

O GOD, our Father, we remember before thee our little sisters of whom thou hast given us charge. We thank thee for the dearness of their friendship and trust. Grant us the insight of love that we may understand them in all their hopes and dreams, their temptations, and discouragements. Endow us with unstudied grace and attractiveness for their sake, with patience and steadfastness in their service, with holiness and the power of prayer. May we realize in each of them the God-given soul, struggling to find itself, and to find thee who art the way, the truth, and the life, that so we may reverence these young lives and may help them to become divine and fair. O thou great Brother, Jesus Christ, give us thy spirit of tender and saving love for these thy little ones, and may our own souls experience thy salvation as we seek to transmit it to others. Accept our petitions, our Father, and fulfil the unspoken desires of our souls, for Jesus' sake.

FOR THE IDLE

O GOD, we remember with pain and pity the thousands of our brothers and sisters who seek honest work and seek in vain. For though the unsatisfied wants of men are many, and though our land is wide and calls for labor, yet these thy sons and daughters have no place to labor, and are turned away in humiliation and despair when they seek it. O righteous God, we acknowledge our common guilt for the disorder of our industry which thrusts even willing workers into the degradation of idleness and want, and teaches some to love the sloth which once they feared and hated.

We remember also with sorrow and compassion the idle rich, who have vigor of body and mind and yet produce no useful thing. Forgive them for loading the burden of their support on the bent shoulders of the working world. Forgive them for wasting in refined excess what would feed the pale children of the poor. Forgive them for setting their poisoned splendor before the thirsty hearts of the young, luring them to theft or shame by the lust of eye and flesh. Forgive them for taking pride in their workless lives and despising those by whose toil they live. Forgive them for appeasing their better self by pretended duties and injurious charities. We beseech thee to awaken them by the new voice of thy Spirit that they may look up into the stern eyes of thy Christ and may be smitten with the blessed pangs of repentance. Grant them strength of soul to rise from their silken shame and to give their brothers a just return of labor for the bread they eat. And to our whole nation do thou grant wisdom to create a world in which none shall be forced to idle in want, and none shall be able to idle in luxury, but in which all shall know the health of wholesome work and the sweetness of well-earned rest.

MORITURI TE SALUTANT

O THOU Eternal One, we who are doomed to die lift up our souls to thee for strength, for Death has passed us in the throng of men and touched us, and we know that at some turn of our pathway he stands waiting to take us by the hand and lead us — we know not whither. We praise thee that to us he is no more an enemy but thy great angel and our friend, who alone can open for some of us the prison-house of pain and misery and set our feet in the roomy spaces of a larger life. Yet we are but children, afraid of the dark and the unknown, and we dread the parting from the life that is so sweet and from the loved ones who are so dear.

Grant us of thy mercy a valiant heart, that we may tread the road with head uplifted and a smiling face. May we do our work to the last with a wholesome joy, and love our loves with an added tenderness because the days of love are short. On thee we cast the heaviest burden that numbs our soul, the gnawing fear for those we love, whom we must leave unsheltered in a selfish world. We trust in thee, for through all our years thou hast been our stay. O thou Father of the fatherless, put thy arm about our little ones! And ere we go, we pray that the days may come when the dying may die unafraid, because men have ceased to prey on the weak, and the great family of the nation enfolds all with its strength and care.

We thank thee that we have tasted the rich life of humanity. We bless thee for every hour of life, for all our share in the joys and strivings of our brothers, for the wisdom gained which will be part of us forever. If soon we must go, yet through thee we have lived and our life flows on in the race. By thy grace we too have helped to shape the future and bring in the better day.

If our spirit droops in loneliness, uphold us by thy companionship. When all the voices of love grow faint and drift away, thy everlasting arms will still be there. Thou art the Father of our spirits; from thee we have come; to thee we go. We rejoice that in the hours of our purer vision, when the pulse-throb of thine eternity is strong within us, we know that no pang of mortality can reach our unconquerable soul, and that for those who abide in thee death is but the gateway to life eternal. Into thy hands we commend our spirit.

PRAYERS OF WRATH

AGAINST WAR

O LORD, since first the blood of Abel cried to thee from the ground that drank it, this earth of thine has been defiled with the blood of man shed by his brother's hand, and the centuries sob with the ceaseless horror of war. Ever the pride of kings and the covetousness of the strong has driven peaceful nations to slaughter. Ever the songs of the past and the pomp of armies have been used to inflame the passions of the people. Our spirit cries out to thee in revolt against it, and we know that our righteous anger is answered by thy holy wrath.

Break thou the spell of the enchantments that make the nations drunk with the lust of battle and draw them on as willing tools of death. Grant us a quiet and steadfast mind when our own nation clamors for vengeance or aggression. Strengthen our sense of justice and our regard for the equal worth of other peoples and races. Grant to the rulers of nations faith in the possibility of peace through justice, and grant to the common people a new and stern enthusiasm for the cause of peace. Bless our soldiers and sailors for their swift obedience and their willingness to answer to the call of duty, but inspire them none the less with a hatred of war, and may they never for love of private glory or advancement provoke its coming. May our young men still rejoice to die for their country with the valor of their fathers, but teach our age nobler methods of matching our strength and more effective ways of giving our life for the flag.

O thou strong Father of all nations, draw all thy great family together with an increasing sense of our common blood and destiny, that peace may come on earth at last, and thy sun may shed its light rejoicing on a holy brotherhood of peoples.

AGAINST ALCOHOLISM

O LORD, we praise thy holy name, for thou hast made bare thine arm in the sight of all nations and done wonders. But still we cry to thee in the weary struggle of our people against the power of drink. Remember, Lord, the strong men who were led astray and blighted in the flower of their youth. Remember the aged who have brought their gray hairs to a dishonored grave. Remember the homes that have been made desolate of joy, the wifely love that has been outraged in its sanctuary, the little children who have learned to despise where once they loved. Remember, O thou great avenger of sin, and make this nation to remember.

May those who now entrap the feet of the weak and make their living by the degradation of men, thrust away their shameful gains and stand clear. But if their conscience is silenced by profit, do thou grant thy people the indomitable strength of faith to make an end of it. May all the great churches of our land shake off those who seek the shelter of religion for that which damns, and stand with level front against their common foe. May all who still soothe their souls with half-truths, saying "Peace, peace," where there can be no peace, learn to see through thy stern eyes and come to the help of Jehovah against the mighty. Help us to cast down the men in high places who use the people's powers to beat back the people's hands from the wrong they fain would crush.

O God, bring nigh the day when all our men shall face their daily task with minds undrugged and with tempered passions; when the unseemly mirth of drink shall seem a shame to all who hear and see; when the trade that debauches men shall be loathed like the trade that debauches women; and when all this black remnant of savagery shall haunt the memory of a new generation but as an evil dream of the night. For this accept our vows, O Lord, and grant thine aid.

AGAINST THE SERVANTS OF MAMMON

WE cry to thee for justice, O Lord, for our soul is weary with the iniquity of greed. Behold the servants of Mammon, who defy thee and drain their fellow men for gain; who grind down the strength of the workers by merciless toil and fling them aside when they are mangled and worn; who rack-rent the poor and make dear the space and air which thou hast made free; who paralyze the hand of justice by corruption and blind the eyes of the people by lies; who nullify by their craft the merciful laws which nobler men have devised for the protection of the weak; who have made us ashamed of our dear country by their defilements and have turned our holy freedom into a hollow name; who have brought upon thy Church the contempt of men and have cloaked their extortion with the gospel of thy Christ.

For the oppression of the poor and the sighing of the needy now do thou arise,

O Lord; for because thou art love, and tender as a mother to the weak, therefore thou art the great hater of iniquity and thy doom is upon those who grow rich on the poverty of the people.

O God, we are afraid, for the thunder-cloud of thy wrath is even now black above us. In the ruins of dead empires we have read how thou hast trodden the wine-press of thine anger when the measure of their sin was full. We are sick at heart when we remember that by the greed of those who enslaved a weaker race that curse was fastened upon us all which still lies black and hopeless across our land, though the blood of a nation was spilled to atone. Save our people from being dragged down into vaster guilt and woe by men who have no vision and know no law except their lust. Shake their souls with awe of thee that they may cease. Help us with clean hands to tear the web which they have woven about us and to turn our people back to thy law, lest the mark of the beast stand out on the right hand and forehead of our nation and our feet be set on the downward path of darkness from which there is no return forever.

AGAINST IMPURITY

O THOU whose light is about me and within me and to whom all things are present, help me this day to keep my life pure in thy sight. Suffer me not by any lawless act of mine to befoul any innocent life or add to the shame and hopelessness of any erring one that struggles faintly against sin. Grant me a steadfast scorn for pleasure bought by human degradation. May no reckless word or wanton look from me kindle the slow fires of wayward passion that will char and consume the divine beauties of any soul. Give me grace to watch over the imaginations of my heart, lest in the unknown hour of my weakness my secret thoughts leap into action and my honor be turned into shame. If my friends trust me with their loved ones, save me from betraying their trust and from slaying the peace of a home. If any dear heart has staked its life and hopes on my love and loyalty, I beseech thee that its joy and strength may never wither through my forgetfulness or guilt. O God, make me pure and a helper to the weak. Grant that even the sins of my past may yield me added wisdom and tenderness to help those who are tempted.

Save our nation from the corruption that breeds corruption. Save our innocent sons and daughters from the secret curse that requites the touch of love with lingering death. O Jesus, thou master of all who are both strong and pure, take our weak and passionate hearts under thy control, that when the dusk settles upon our life, we may go to our long rest with no pang of shame, and may enter into the blessedness of seeing God, which thou hast promised only to the pure in heart.

THE PROGRESS OF HUMANITY

FOR THE KINGDOM OF GOD

O CHRIST, thou hast bidden us pray for the coming of thy Father's kingdom, in which his righteous will shall be done on earth. We have treasured thy words, but we have forgotten their meaning, and thy great hope has grown dim in thy Church. We bless thee for the inspired souls of all ages who saw afar the shining city of God, and by faith left the profit of the present to follow their vision. We rejoice that today the hope of these lonely hearts is becoming the clear faith of millions. Help us, O Lord, in the courage of faith to seize what has now come so near, that the glad day of God may dawn at last. As we have mastered Nature that we might gain wealth, help us now to master the social relations of mankind that we may gain justice and a world of brothers. For what shall it profit our nation if it gain numbers and riches, and lose the sense of the living God and the joy of human brotherhood?

Make us determined to live by truth and

not by lies, to found our common life on the eternal foundations of righteousness and love, and no longer to prop the tottering house of wrong by legalized cruelty and force. Help us to make the welfare of all the supreme law of our land, that so our commonwealth may be built strong and secure on the love of all its citizens. Cast down the throne of Mammon who ever grinds the life of men, and set up thy throne, O Christ, for thou didst die that men might live. Show thy erring children at last the way from the City of Destruction to the City of Love, and fulfil the longings of the prophets of humanity. Our Master, once more we make thy faith our prayer: "Thy kingdom come! Thy will be done on earth!"

A SOCIAL LITANY

Used at a Mass Meeting under the Auspices of the Joint Commission on Social Service at the General Convention of the Protestant Episcopal Church, New York, 1913.

From the sins that divide us, from all class bitterness and race hatred, from forgetfulness of thee and indifference to our fellow-men:

Good Lord, deliver us.

From the corruption of the franchise and of civil government, from greed and from the arbitrary love of power:

Good Lord, deliver us.

From the fear of unemployment and the evils of overwork, from the curse of child-labor and the ill-paid toil of women:

Good Lord, deliver us.

From the luxury that enervates, from the poverty that stultifies:

Good Lord, deliver us.

That it may please thee to unite the inhabitants of every city, state and nation in the bonds of peace and concord:

First Published by "THE SURVEY." Used by permission.

We beseech thee to hear us, Good Lord.

That thy followers may be strong to achieve industrial justice, and to bid the oppressed go free:

We beseech thee to hear us, Good Lord.

That the labor movement may be confirmed in disinterested honor, and that the employers of labor may fashion their dealings according to the laws of equity:

We beseech thee to hear us, Good Lord.

That thou wilt help us to give all men health of body and soul:

We beseech thee to hear us, Good Lord.

That the watchword of the Christian State, "Thou shalt love thy neighbor as thyself," may become a command with power:

We beseech thee to hear us, Good Lord.

That the spirit of reconciliation may be made manifest among men:

We beseech thee to hear us, Good Lord.

That it may please thee to inspire thy Church with the vision of the New Jerusalem coming down from heaven to men, and that thy Kingdom may come on earth:

We beseech thee to hear us, Good Lord.

The grace of our Lord Jesus Christ, and the love of God, and the fellowship of the Holy Spirit be with us all evermore. Amen.

FOR THOSE WHO COME AFTER US

O GOD, we pray thee for those who come after us, for our children, and the children of our friends, and for all the young lives that are marching up from the gates of birth, pure and eager, with the morning sunshine on their faces. We remember with a pang that these will live in the world we are making for them. We are wasting the resources of the earth in our headlong greed, and they will suffer want. We are building sunless houses and joyless cities for our profit, and they must dwell therein. We are making the burden heavy and the pace of work pitiless, and they will fall wan and sobbing by the wayside. We are poisoning the air of our land by our lies and our uncleanness, and they will breathe it.

O God, thou knowest how we have cried out in agony when the sins of our fathers have been visited upon us, and how we have struggled vainly against the inexorable fate that coursed in our blood or bound us in a prison-house of life. Save us from maiming the innocent ones who come after us by the added cruelty of our sins. Help us to break the ancient force of evil by a holy and steadfast will and to endow our children with purer blood and nobler thoughts. Grant us grace to leave the earth fairer than we found it; to build upon it cities of God in which the cry of needless pain shall cease; and to put the yoke of Christ upon our business life that it may serve and not destroy. Lift the veil of the future and show us the generation to come as it will be if blighted by our guilt, that our lust may be cooled and we may walk in the fear of the Eternal. Grant us a vision of the far-off years as they may be if redeemed by the sons of God, that we may take heart and do battle for thy children and ours.

ON THE HARM WE HAVE DONE

OUR Father, we look back on the years that are gone and shame and sorrow come upon us, for the harm we have done to others rises up in our memory to accuse us. Some we have seared with the fire of our lust, and some we have scorched by the heat of our anger. In some we helped to quench the glow of young ideals by our selfish pride and craft, and in some we have nipped the opening bloom of faith by the frost of our unbelief.

We might have followed thy blessed footsteps, O Christ, binding up the bruised hearts of our brothers and guiding the wayward passions of the young to firmer manhood. Instead, there are poor hearts now broken and darkened because they encountered us on the way, and some perhaps remember us only as the beginning of their misery or sin.

O God, we know that all our prayers can never bring back the past, and no tears can wash out the red marks with which we have scarred some life that stands before our memory with accusing eyes. Grant that at least a humble and pure life may grow out of our late contrition, that in the brief days still left to us we may comfort and heal where we have scorned and crushed. Change us by the power of thy saving grace from sources of evil into forces for good, that with all our strength we may fight the wrongs we have aided, and aid the right we have clogged. Grant us this boon, that for every harm we have done, we may do some brave act of salvation, and that for every soul that has stumbled or fallen through us, we may bring to thee some other weak or despairing one, whose strength has been renewed by our love, that so the face of thy Christ may smile upon us and the light within us may shine undimmed.

FOR THE PROPHETS AND PIONEERS

WE praise thee, Almighty God, for thine elect, the prophets and martyrs of humanity, who gave their thoughts and prayers and agonies for the truth of God and the freedom of the people. We praise thee that amid loneliness and the contempt of men, in poverty and imprisonment, when they were condemned by the laws of the mighty and buffeted on the scaffold, thou didst uphold them by thy spirit in loyalty to thy holy cause.

Our hearts burn within us as we follow the bleeding feet of thy Christ down the centuries, and count the mounts of anguish on which he was crucified anew in his prophets and the true apostles of his spirit. Help us to forgive those who did it, for some truly thought they were serving thee when they suppressed thy light, but oh, save us from the same mistake! Grant us an unerring instinct for what is right and true, and a swift sympathy to divine those who truly love and serve the people. Suffer us not by thoughtless condemnation or selfish opposition to weaken the arm and chill the spirit of those who strive for the redemption of mankind. May we never bring upon us the blood of all the righteous by renewing the spirit of those who persecuted them in the past. Grant us rather that we, too, may be counted in the chosen band of those who have given their life as a ransom for the many. Send us forth with the pathfinders of humanity to lead thy people another day's march toward the land of promise.

And if we, too, must suffer loss, and drink of the bitter pool of misunderstanding and scorn, uphold us by thy Spirit in steadfastness and joy because we are found worthy to share in the work and the reward of Jesus and all the saints.

FOR THOSE WITHOUT KNOWLEDGE

O THOU Eternal One, we adore thee who in all ages hast been the great companion and teacher of mankind; for thou hast lifted our race from the depths, and hast made us to share in thy conscious intelligence and thy will that makes for righteousness and love. Thou alone art our Redeemer, for thy lifting arms were about us and thy persistent voice was in our hearts as we slowly climbed up from savage darkness and cruelty. Thou knowest how often we have resisted thee and loved the easy ways of sin rather than the toilsome gain of self-control and the divine irritation of thy truth.

O God, visit not upon us the guilt of the past, for our fathers have slain thy prophets. They silenced the voices that spoke thine onward thought, and generations have perished in soddenness and misery because the strong once quenched the light of truth. Do thou free humanity at last from the blood-rusted chains with which the past still binds us. Multiply the God-conquered souls who open their hearts gladly to the light that makes us free, for all creation shall be in travail till these sons of God attain their glory.

We pray thee for those who amid all the knowledge of our day are still without knowledge; for those who hear not the sighs of the children that toil, nor the sobs of such as are wounded because others have made haste to be rich; for those who have never felt the hot tears of the mothers of the poor that struggle vainly against poverty and vice. Arouse them, we beseech thee, from their selfish comfort and grant them the grace of social repentance. Smite us all with the conviction that for us ignorance is sin, and that we are indeed our brother's keeper if our own hand has helped to lay him low. Though increase of knowledge bring increase of sorrow, may we turn without flinching to the light and offer ourselves as instruments of thy spirit in bringing order and beauty out of disorder and darkness.

FOR A SHARE IN THE WORK OF REDEMPTION

O GOD, thou great Redeemer of mankind, our hearts are tender in the thought of thee, for in all the afflictions of our race thou hast been afflicted, and in the sufferings of thy people it was thy body that was crucified. Thou hast been wounded by our transgressions and bruised by our iniquities, and all our sins are laid at last on thee. Amid the groaning of creation we behold thy spirit in travail till the sons of God shall be born in freedom and holiness.

We pray thee, O Lord, for the graces of a pure and holy life that we may no longer add to the dark weight of the world's sin that is laid upon thee, but may share with thee in thy redemptive work. As we have thirsted with evil passions to the destruction of men, do thou fill us now with hunger and thirst for justice that we may bear glad tidings to the poor and set at liberty all who are in the prison-house of want and sin.

Lay thy Spirit upon us and inspire us with a passion of Christlike love that we may join our lives to the weak and oppressed and may strengthen their cause by bearing their sorrows. And if the evil that is threatened turns to smite us and if we must learn the dark malignity of sinful power, comfort us by the thought that thus we are bearing in our body the marks of Jesus, and that only those who share in his free sacrifice shall feel the plenitude of thy life. Help us in patience to carry forward the eternal cross of thy Christ, counting it joy if we, too, are sown as grains of wheat in the furrows of the world, for only by the agony of the righteous comes redemption.

FOR THE CHURCH

O GOD, we pray for thy Church, which is set today amid the perplexities of a changing order, and face to face with a great new task. We remember with love the nurture she gave to our spiritual life in its infancy, the tasks she set for our growing strength, the influence of the devoted hearts she gathers, the steadfast power for good she has exerted. When we compare her with all other human institutions, we rejoice, for there is none like her. But when we judge her by the mind of her Master, we bow in pity and contrition. Oh, baptize her afresh in the life-giving spirit of Jesus! Grant her a new birth, though it be with the travail of repentance and humiliation. Bestow upon her a more imperious responsiveness to duty, a swifter compassion with suffering, and an utter loyalty to the will of God. Put upon her lips the ancient gospel of her Lord. Help her to proclaim boldly the coming of the kingdom of God and the doom of all that resist it. Fill her with the prophets' scorn of tyranny, and with a Christlike tenderness for the heavy-laden and down-trodden. Give her faith to espouse the cause of the people, and in their hands that grope after freedom and light to recognize the bleeding hands of the Christ. Bid her cease from seeking her own life, lest she lose it. Make her valiant to give up her life to humanity, that like her crucified Lord she may mount by the path of the cross to a higher glory.

FOR OUR CITY

O GOD, we pray thee for this, the city of our love and pride. We rejoice in her spacious beauty and her busy ways of commerce, in her stores and factories where hand joins hand in toil, and in her blessed homes where heart joins heart for rest and love.

Help us to make our city the mighty common workshop of our people, where every one will find his place and task, in daily achievement building up his own life to resolute manhood, keen to do his best with hand and mind. Help us to make our city the greater home of our people, where all may live their lives in comfort, unafraid, loving their loves in peace and rounding out their years in strength.

Bind our citizens, not by the bond of money and of profit alone, but by the glow of neighborly good will, by the thrill of common joys, and the pride of common possessions. As we set the greater aims for the future of our city, may we ever remember that her true wealth and greatness consist, not in the abundance of the things we possess, but in the justice of her institutions and the brotherhood of her children. Make her rich in her sons and daughters and famous through the lofty passions that inspire them.

We thank thee for the patriot men and women of the past whose generous devotion to the common good has been the making of our city. Grant that our own generation may build worthily on the foundation they have laid. If in the past there have been some who have sold the city's good for private gain, staining her honor by their cunning and greed, fill us, we beseech thee, with the righteous anger of true sons that we may purge out the shame lest it taint the future years.

Grant us a vision of our city, fair as she might be: a city of justice, where none shall prey on others; a city of plenty, where vice and poverty shall cease to fester; a city of brotherhood, where all success shall be founded on service, and honor shall be given to nobleness alone; a city of peace, where order shall not rest on force, but on the love of all for the city, the great mother of the common life and weal. Hear thou, O Lord, the silent prayer of all our hearts as we each pledge our time and strength and thought to speed the day of her coming beauty and righteousness.

FOR THE COOPERATIVE COMMONWEALTH

O GOD, we praise thee for the dream of the golden city of peace and righteousness which has ever haunted the prophets of humanity, and we rejoice with joy unspeakable that at last the people have conquered the freedom and knowledge and power which may avail to turn into reality the vision that so long has beckoned in vain.

Speed now the day when the plains and the hills and the wealth thereof shall be the people's own, and thy freemen shall not live as tenants of men on the earth which thou hast given to all; when no babe shall be born without its equal birthright in the riches and knowledge wrought out by the labor of the ages; and when the mighty engines of industry shall throb with a gladder music because the men who ply these great tools shall be their owners and masters.

Bring to an end, O Lord, the inhumanity of the present, in which all men are ridden by the pale fear of want while the nation of which they are citizens sits throned amid the wealth of their making; when the manhood in some is cowed by helplessness, while the soul of others is surfeited and sick with power which no frail son of the dust should wield.

O God, save us, for our nation is at strife with its own soul and is sinning against the light which thou aforetime hast kindled in it. Thou hast called our people to freedom, but we are withholding from men their share in the common heritage without which freedom becomes a hollow name. Thy Christ has kindled in us the passion for brotherhood, but the social life we have built, denies and slays brotherhood.

We pray thee to revive in us the hardy spirit of our forefathers that we may establish and complete their work, building on the basis of their democracy the firm edifice of a cooperative commonwealth, in which both government and industry shall be of the people, by the people, and for the people. May we, who now live, see the oncoming of the great day of God, when all men shall stand side by side in equal worth and real freedom, all toiling and all reaping, masters of nature but brothers of men, exultant in the tide of the common life, and jubilant in the adoration of Thee, the source of their blessings and the Father of all.

FOR CONFERENCES AND CONVENTIONS

FIRST DAY

O GOD, we praise thy holy name, for thou hast brought us from afar, drawn together by the splendor of thy Kingdom, to take counsel for thy work. Be with us through all the strain of the days that are before us. Brood over our assemblies with thy Holy Spirit. Give us vision beyond the range of worldly prudence, and by thy wisdom make us wise, lest all our planning be futile. If difficulties confront us, give us the courageous faith that bids the mountains melt away. Smite a pathway even across the impassable sea for thy people. Hush all spirit of contention and self-will. Make us peaceful through love and through the unity of our desire. May this gathering set the standard of our Lord high up where in coming years we may see it and take courage to fulfil the vows we here make.

Through thee we send our benediction to our loved ones afar, to the dear people in our

Used by permission of "THE WOMAN'S PRESS."

own homes, and to the Associations in whose name we have come here.

We remember with reverent love our friends and fellow workers who rest from their labor and now behold thee face to face. May the life of our heroic dead still be a living force among us, through the characters they have moulded and through thy Holy Spirit which binds in one the Church militant and the Church triumphant.

Thy peace be upon this city, and upon all who love the Lord Jesus. In His name we pray.

SECOND DAY

AS we look across the vast field of our work, O Master, we feel the challenge of thy call and turn to thee for strength. So much to do for thee, and so little wherewith to do it!

O Christ, thou who art touched with a feeling of our infirmities and hast been tempted even as we, look with thy great sympathy on thy servants. Thou knowest the drain of our daily work and the limitations of our bodies. Thou knowest that we carry but a little candle of knowledge to guide the feet of the erring amid the mazes of modern life. Thou knowest that our longing for holiness of heart is frustrated by the drag of our earthliness and the weight of ancient sins.

Fit us for our work, lest we fail thee. We lean on thee, thou great giver of life, and pray for physical vigor and quiet strength. We call to thee, thou fountain of light, to flood our minds with thy radiance and to make all things clear and simple. We submit our inmost desires to thy holy will, and beseech thee to make thy law sweet to our willing hearts.

Give, Lord, what thou askest, and then ask what thou wilt. We make our prayer, O God, by faith in Christ, our Lord.

THIRD DAY

WE praise thee, O God, for our friends and fellow workers, for the touch of their hands and the brightness of their faces, for the cheer of their words and the outflow of good will that refreshes us.

Grant us the insight of love that we may see them as thou seest, not as frail mortals, but as radiant children of God who have wrought patience out of tribulation and who bear in earthen vessels the treasures of thy grace.

May nought mar the joy of our fellowship here. May none remain lonely and hungry of heart among us. Let none go hence without the joy of new friendships. Give us more capacity for love and a richer consciousness of being loved. Overcome our coldness and reserve that we may throw ajar the gates of our heart and keep open house this day.

Lift our human friendships to the level of spiritual companionship. May we realize thee as the eternal bond of our unity. Shine upon us from the faces of thy servants, thou all-pervading beauty, that in loving them we may be praising thee. Through Christ, our Lord.

FOURTH DAY (SUNDAY)

ON this Day of our Lord and in his sight I will make a fresh affirmation of my faith.

I affirm my faith in the reality of the spiritual world, in the sacred voice of duty, in the compelling power of truth and holiness, in prayer, in the life eternal, in Him who is the life of my life and the reality behind all things visible. I rejoice to believe in God.

I reaffirm my discipleship and the dedication of my body and mind to Jesus Christ, my Lord. I claim anew a share in his redemption and full salvation. As he has been my Saviour to this day, so shall he be my Saviour to the end. I merge all the power of my life in his redemptive purpose and stand ready to bear the cross after him.

I affirm my faith in the kingdom of God and my hope in its final triumph. I determine by faith to live day by day within the higher order and the divine peace of my true fatherland, and to carry its spirit and laws into all my dealings in the world that now is.

I make an act of love toward all my fellow men. I accept them as they are, with all their sins and failures, and declare my solidarity with them. If any have wronged or grieved me, I place my mind within the all-comprehending and all-loving mind of God, and here and now forgive. I desire to minister God's love to men and to offer no hindrance to the free flow of his love through me.

I affirm my faith in life. I call life good and not evil. I accept the limitations of my own life and believe it is possible for me to live a beautiful and Christlike life within the conditions set for me. Through the power of Christ which descends on me, which besets me behind and before, and which dwells in the innermost fastnesses of my spirit, I know that I can be more than conqueror.

FIFTH DAY

OUR Father, amid the cheer and comfort of these days we remember those who suffer.

We pray for all who are sick and in pain, especially the sick whom we know and love.

We pray for all whose homes have been visited by death, and for those who hear his footfall drawing nigh.

We pray for those who are out of work and for all whose age is burdened by fear of want.

We pray for all lonely and homeless and unloved people.

We pray for workers who are underpaid or whose work is grinding and barren of pleasure and hope.

We pray for all who suffer by the war, for the soldiers in danger, for the wounded, for the widowed and fatherless, and for those in fear and foreboding of loss.

We pray for all who are tempted by evil men or women, and for all who are weak and foolish and wayward.

We pray for all whose inner light has been quenched and who walk in the darkness of doubt and the cold of unbelief.

We pray for all religious and social workers who are discouraged and losing faith.

O Lord, thou hast been our own refuge and a present help in trouble. In our weakness we have felt thy might and in our loneliness thy love. In all our afflictions thou art afflicted, thou great Shepherd, and thou wilt not rest till these lost ones are gathered and comforted. We stand in the sight of the cross and know that the sin and sorrow of the world lie on thee. May we take our share of it willingly, as members of the body of Christ. We make our prayer in his name.

LAST DAY

OUR Father, as we come to the parting, we humbly give thee thanks for the days of our gathering. We thank thee for the real work accomplished, for the plans laid, for the officers chosen, and we beseech thee to set thy seal beneath what we have done and make it valid.

We thank thee for the quickening of old friendships, for new and fruitful contacts, and for the broadened understanding of our common work. We pray thee for fresh devotion to the great aims and possibilities of our Association, for unfeigned love for our fellow workers, and for a deep and Christlike longing to save and ennoble the girls and women whose lives we touch. Make us worthy to bear thy message. May every word and act be the simple pulsing of a Christian heart.

We thank thee for the voices that have interpreted thy will and summoned us to thy work. We praise thee for the hours of holy quiet in which we crossed the threshold of thy presence and listened to the inner voice in the most holy place. Fix on the sensitive film of our spirits the image and splendor of Christ which shone upon us in the great moments of these past days.

And now, as we turn our faces homeward toward the toil and care, the trials and temptations of our work, we feel our utter need of thee thou great companion of our souls. Be thou the strength of our weakness, the wisdom of our foolishness, the triumph of our failures, the changeless unity in our changing days. Knowing the brevity of our years, help us to work resolutely while it is day. Shine upon us, thou sun of our life, even in the valley of the shadow, and may the song of faith never die in our hearts. We make our petition through Jesus Christ, our Saviour and Lord.

THE AUTHOR'S PRAYER

O Thou who art the light of my soul, I thank Thee for the incomparable joy of listening to thy voice within, and I know that no word of thine shall return void, however brokenly uttered. If aught in this book was said through lack of knowledge, or through weakness of faith in Thee or of love for men, I pray Thee to overrule my sin and turn aside its force before it harm thy cause. Pardon the frailty of thy servant, and look upon him only as he sinks his life in Jesus, his Master and Saviour. Amen.